Dragonfly
A CHILDHOOD MEMOIR

Also by W. Nikola-Lisa

America: My Land, Your Land, Our Land
Bein' With You This Way
Can You Top That?
How We Are Smart
Magic in the Margins
My Teacher Can Teach...*Anyone!*
No Babies Asleep
One Hole in the Road
Setting the Turkeys Free
Shake Dem Halloween Bones
Storm
Summer Sun Risin'
Tangletalk
The Year With Grandma Moses
Till Year's Good End
To Hear the Angels Sing

W. Nikola-Lisa

Dragonfly
A CHILDHOOD MEMOIR

Gyroscope Books
Chicago

Text Copyright © 2010 by W. Nikola-Lisa

All rights reserved.
No part of this book may be reproduced or transmitted in any form or by any means, electronic or mechanical, including photocopying, recording, or by any information storage and retrieval system, without the written permission of the Publisher, except where permitted by law.

Library of Congress Info
Author: Nikola-Lisa, W. [American, b.1951]
Summary: The author reflects on his childhood growing up in a small cattle town in south Texas.

ISBN-10: 0-9972524-2-1
ISBN-13: 978-0-9972524-2-2
LCCN: 2010902187

Published by
Gyroscope Books
Chicago

To Dorothy, for her courage

As memory may be a paradise from which we cannot be driven, it may also be a hell from which we cannot escape.

— John Lancaster Spalding

South Texas
Early 1960s

Chapter One

I REMEMBER the first time I met Craig.

We were in his backyard. He was holding a dragonfly in his hands—one set of double wings in his left hand, the other set in his right.

He kept the wings taut, stretched to their fullest.

The dragonfly twitched and buzzed, trying to escape its captor.

Slowly, Craig raised his prey to the sunlight and inspected it—the silvery, translucent wings, the bluish-green body, the large, bulbous eyes. Then he lowered it and began to pull his hands apart.

The dragonfly buzzed louder.

But Craig continued to pull his hands apart. He pulled until the dragonfly's left wings gave way. They ripped from its body with a snap that sent a chill down my spine.

Craig dropped the dragonfly's body. It lay on the ground twitching, drawing a circle with its body as it batted the only set of wings it had left.

"Here," he said, handing me the wings he held in his left hand.

Then he turned and walked away.

I stared at the dragonfly on the ground. It hardly twitched now, exhausted by its own frenetic activity.

I watched it for a moment or two, until it lay completely still. Then I leaned over and lay the set of wings I held next to its body.

In its stillness the dragonfly looked peaceful, but like many things in my life the truth of it was quite different.

Chapter Two

IT WAS a hot summer day. After lunch I crossed the county road that separated my house from Craig's and walked up his driveway.

Like most ranch-style houses, there are always two doors of entry: the formal front door, with a walkway off the asphalt drive; and the back door, which could either be on the side of the house or around back.

Craig's second door was around back.

You walked up the driveway, through the carport, and around to the back of the house to get to it. The backyard had a tree, a play area, and lots of grass, carpet grass. I never understood why they called it "carpet grass." Ours was rough and splotchy with weeds. Hardly the kind of carpet you'd want to lie down on.

I knocked on the door. Craig's mom answered in that super-sweet way she always did—"Hello, dear, looking for Craig?"

"Yes, ma'am," I replied.

"He's in his room," she said, holding the door open.

I walked through the kitchen, took a right down the hallway, and walked to the last room on the left. The door was closed, so I knocked.

"Yeah, who is it?" a gruff voice replied.

"It's me," I said.

"Door's open," the voice answered.

When I entered the room, Craig was lying on the covers of his bed, fully clothed, holding his pellet gun. Craig was the only one of my friends who had a pellet gun powered by a CO_2 cartridge. Most of my friends, me included, owned a cheaper and less powerful air-pumped BB gun.

I said hello again, but Craig ignored me. Instead

he raised the pellet gun and shot at one of the airplane models displayed on the top shelf of his bureau.

"Well, what do you want?" he asked, as flecks of plastic sprayed the floor beside me.

"Uh, do you want to play?" I asked, sheepishly.

"Play? What do you think I'm doing?" he replied, taking a shot at another airplane model.

"You know, play outside," I said, jamming my hands into my pockets.

"Yeah, okay," he said after awhile, swinging his legs out of bed. "Why not?"

Chapter Three

I DON'T know if we ever made it outside to play or not. If we did, our play was uneventful—though not necessarily uninteresting.

There was plenty to do. We hunted. We fished. Rode our bikes. Built forts. You know, the usual things boys like to do.

So even though our play that day might not have been eventful, it was certainly not uninteresting. What usually kept things interesting, even eventful, was Craig.

He was different from the rest of my friends. He possessed a certain "knowing" that my other friends lacked. I wouldn't say it was wisdom. Far from it.

But he possessed something—or, perhaps, more accurately, he was possessed by something.

Not long after the dragonfly incident I was home with Mom, cleaning up after breakfast. While I cleared the table, Mom washed dishes.

No matter the chore, she usually did it with gusto—and she sang.

Mom loved to sing.

Lots of times when I came home from school she'd be singing away—songs by Irving Berlin, Cole Porter, Rodgers and Hammerstein.

She liked all kinds of music, and she really liked Johnny Cash. She sang all of his songs. Her favorite song was *Ring of Fire*, and she sang it just the way Cash did, low and bassy.

I loved singing *Ring of Fire*, too, trying to copy Cash's deep, throaty sound. But it's not Johnny Cash, or even Mom, that I associate with the song—it's Craig.

As Mom stood at the kitchen sink, she glanced up and saw Craig and his three younger sisters playing in the brush on the side of their house.

As she looked closer, Mom dropped the pan she was washing and gasped.

Craig had herded his sisters together and was pouring a ring of gasoline around them.

Before Mom could move, Craig lit the gas with a match. The brush crackled with fire, sending small plumes of purple-blue smoke into the air. As the brush crackled, Craig's sisters screamed.

Mom picked up the telephone and called Craig's house. She could hardly speak. All that came out of her panicked voice was:

"Hurry...

   Outside...

      Craig...

         Fire!"

But that was enough. Within a minute or two the housekeeper ran outside, dashed through the crackling ring of fire, and led the girls to safety.

Craig just stood there, the corners of his mouth pulled back into the faintest hint of a smile.

Chapter Four

CRAIG WASN'T the only firebug, though.

I don't know why, but all of my friends loved playing with fire. Maybe it was just a boy's thing. In any case, it usually got us into trouble.

That was the case at one of our forts one day, our favorite fort of the many we had in the neighborhood. It was in the middle of a grove of trees behind the dentist's house.

Most of the trees in south Texas are mesquite trees. They're short and stubby, and have really sharp thorns. You don't build forts in mesquite trees.

I don't know what kind of trees were in the grove, but they were perfect for building a large fort.

And that's what we did.

We created "rooms" all over the grove, by tying tree branches together, or stacking up dead branches, or just by marking out a space with a ring of stones.

And we dug a fire pit.

We spent hours in this fort, imagining we were lost, stranded on some remote island.

And, often, to wile away the time, we'd light a fire in the fire pit. If we didn't have anything to cook, we'd just sit and poke the flames with a stick.

One afternoon my friend Tad and I decided to play in the fort. As we approached the stand of trees, we saw Craig coming out of the main entrance of the fort.

We crouched in the weeds so he wouldn't see us and watched him walk along the tree line toward his house. Craig was our friend, but we didn't always want to play with him.

When we got to the fort we noticed some embers smoldering in the fire pit. Craig must have started a fire but didn't put it out completely.

Seeing the embers, Tad and I went to work. We got on our hands and knees and began blowing into the heap of ashes until it burst into flames. Then we piled on twigs, and, when those caught fire, larger branches until we had a steady fire.

We were proud of ourselves—until the fire jumped the pit and set the surrounding brush on fire.

The fire took off quickly.

We swatted at it, stamped on it, threw dirt on it, even spat at it, but nothing we did could tame the spreading flames.

Finally, we ran as fast as we could back to my house hoping no one would see us.

By the time we reached the driveway, we could see smoke spiraling above the grove of trees. In the distance we heard the shrill of a fire truck's siren.

Within minutes a fire truck pulled up next to the open field that led to the burning stand of trees. Doors flew open and several men jumped out.

After surveying the situation, they jumped back into the truck and drove across the field toward the clump of trees belching smoke.

About midway through the field the fire truck

ground to a halt. It was stuck in the sand that makes up most of south Texas.

By now a crowd had gathered to watch.

It was late afternoon and parents were getting home from work. The dentist and his wife looked on from their house. The doctor watched with his wife and children from their backyard.

Mom and my sisters noticed the commotion and joined Tad and me at the end of the driveway.

And then there was Craig.

Since Craig's house was closest to the field, Craig and his father, Harold, walked up to the road to talk with the county deputy who had just pulled up.

We couldn't hear what they were talking about, but we could see Harold talking with the deputy, and then with Craig, and then with the deputy again, and then with Craig.

Then, all of a sudden, Harold grabbed Craig by the arm and started walloping him on the behind. He kept walloping him as he dragged him into the house.

"Oh, that Craig," Mom said after awhile, "he sure does stir up trouble."

"He sure does," I said under my breath, suppressing a smile.

Chapter Five

CRAIG, LIKE his father, could be very cold and stern. He seemed to enjoy bullying us around, being the tough guy. So, seeing him stuck in a tree made us all giggle a little.

It happened one day when we were climbing one of the taller trees behind our house. We often climbed it when there was nothing else to do.

Sue, my middle sister, was the best climber. I was pretty good, too—better than Tad.

Craig didn't like to climb trees. I think he was afraid of heights, though he'd never admit it.

But on this day he clambered up the tree like the rest of us, and to our surprise made it all the way to the top.

Then he froze.

He just sat there, hugging the tree trunk with his arms, holding on for dear life. Sue and I tried everything to get him to come down.

We'd scamper up the trunk, talk to him for a few minutes, then head down, saying, "Come on, Craig, come on down with us."

He'd just clutch the trunk tighter, shake his head, and mumble something we couldn't understand.

"But it's easy as cake," we'd say, and then scramble down the tree to show him that, in fact, it was pretty easy.

But nothing we did or said could budge Craig. He just sat there, petrified.

After a while, Tad spied an irrigation pipe in the weeds beside our house. We dragged the pipe to the tree, stood it on end, and pushed it so it landed against the trunk right next to Craig.

All Craig had to do was reach out, hold onto the pipe with both hands, swing his leg over, and WHOSH he'd be down in a second.

But, no, not Craig. He ignored the pipe, ignored

us. He even ignored Mom when she walked up to see what was going on.

"Craig's in the tree," I said.

"Yeah, he climbed way up and now he's stuck," Sue chimed in.

Mom craned her head back, shielded her eyes from the afternoon sun, and looked up at Craig.

What a pitiful sight, Craig sitting there clinging to the tree trunk, whimpering, as we watched from below.

That's when Craig's father showed up. Harold had just got home from work and saw the ruckus in our yard, so he came over.

"What's going on?" he asked.

"It looks like Craig's got himself stuck in the tree," Mom replied.

"Hmmph," Harold snorted, looking up.

Then, without warning, he shouted in the deepest, darkest voice I'd ever heard: "Craig, get down from that tree—*NOW!*"

Craig's back stiffened. He grabbed the pipe,

swung his leg around it, and slid down like it was the fire pole at the fire station.

But there was no fire truck waiting at the bottom of the pole. Only Harold, who grabbed Craig's arm, jerked him to his feet, and dragged him home.

We stood there looking at each other. No one said a word. Then we turned and walked back to our house.

Chapter Six

ALONG WITH making forts, riding bikes, and climbing trees, we hunted.

In Texas almost every kid had a couple of guns. Not just BB guns or pellet guns, but shotguns and rifles. For us, hunting was like breathing. You did it from a young age.

Craig and I often hunted in my backyard. We had a row of trees along the west side of our property that acted as a pretty good bird blind.

Just about everyday at sundown a flock of doves flew over those trees. Knowing this, we'd set up and wait for them—me, Craig, and Mom.

At twelve years old, I was just a bit too young to

use a shotgun by myself. And Mom would never let me use it alone with Craig.

There was a good reason for this.

One day, while we were shooting doves in my backyard, Craig forgot a cardinal rule.

The rule was pretty clear: if you weren't shooting, you lowered your gun barrel and kneeled while the other person took his turn.

The way it worked was simple.

Mom sat in a chair. I stood on one side of her and Craig on the other side.

When I was shooting, Craig kneeled and waited his turn. When Craig shot, I kneeled and waited my turn.

It all went like clockwork—until Craig forgot the rule.

It was my turn to shoot, so I was standing ready for the doves to come over the trees. Craig was kneeling next to Mom, gun lowered, waiting his turn.

All of a sudden, there was a rush of wings and a bevy of doves darted over the trees—twenty or thirty of them. In the excitement, Craig raised his gun to shoot.

As the gun came up, Mom, sensing the danger, swung her arm around towards Craig. There was a loud THUD as her forearm hit the barrel of the gun, followed by an even louder BANG as the gun fired.

There was an eerie quiet afterwards.

Mom, a nurse by training, quickly assessed the situation and, seeing that no one was hurt, let her emotions go. Her fists clenched, her face contorted, and she screamed as loud as I'd ever heard her scream before: *C-r-a-i-g!*

I don't remember dove hunting with Craig too much after that.

Chapter Seven

ALTHOUGH HUNTING was a big part of my life and a big part of the culture of south Texas, it didn't come natural to me. I had to learn it.

Before I got my first gun, I had a slingshot.

That's usually how it went: you carried a stick, threw some stones, graduated to a slingshot, then a knife, and finally you got a gun, all by the time you were twelve.

I remember the first time I used a slingshot.

I was in Craig's backyard, waiting for him to come out of his house. I was excited to show off the slingshot.

While I waited for him, I began filling my pockets with rocks. As I did this, a bird flew by and landed on a tree branch not far from me. I watched it flitter among the branches, until it perched on the topmost branch.

Quietly, I took a rock out of my pocket, placed it in the slingshot, and pulled it back. Then, taking aim, I let go of the leather thong that held the rock.

To my surprise—*and horror*—I hit the bird right in the middle of its back.

"Surprise" because I couldn't believe that I hit the first thing that I had aimed at.

"Horror" because the bird fell out of the tree and landed at my feet, its body shuddering with agony until it lay motionless before me.

I had tasted my first "kill," but what a mixture of delight and regret.

Chapter Eight

MY INITIATION into gun culture was inevitable. Every kid in south Texas experiences it at some point.

And it wasn't just our parents teaching us about guns. We learned a lot about gun culture watching television, especially B-rated Westerns like *A Lust to Kill* and *Rio Bravo*.

But it wasn't B-rated Western movies that I learned from the most. It was the television series *The Rifleman*.

Who could forget Chuck Connors playing Lucas McCain, shooting bad guys with his modified rapid-fire Winchester? And always from the hip—*pow-pow-pow-pow-pow-pow-pow-pow!*

All of us—Craig and Tad and me—imagined

that we were the tall, rugged gunslinger-turned-homesteader we saw on television each week.

We knew most of the episodes by heart. *The Rifleman* was in our blood. It shaped the way we saw the world. The way we interacted with each other.

So, it's no wonder that Craig shot me.

It happened one Saturday afternoon. Craig and I were in a tiff, a really bad one—who knows over what. We stood in my front yard, squared off against each other, red-hot mad—Craig holding his pellet gun; me clenching my fists.

Now if I had any sense I should have walked away. Craig with a gun was not to be taken lightly. But instead of walking away, I took a step forward. That's because Craig dared me to. You know, just like on *The Rifleman,* "Take one more step, and I'll shoot you!"

When I heard those words it was as if I was on autopilot: I just took that step (I'd seen it done a hundred times before). Craig must have been thinking *Rifleman,* too, because as soon as I took a step he swung his gun up, hip-high, and pulled the trigger.

The pellet hit me square in the palm of my hand.

If it had hit me anywhere else it would have glanced off of me. It would have stung, but it wouldn't have broken the skin. But the palm is soft and fleshy, and the pellet broke the skin.

I winced with pain, turned, and ran into the house. Now, that should have been the end of it, except my sister was home.

Sue was a tomboy and my special protector. When I ran away from home, Sue came and got me. If I needed help fixing my bike, it was Sue who helped me.

I must have run to her crying because the next thing I know she's tearing out of the house, chasing Craig.

She caught him at the edge of our yard, before he crossed the road into his yard. She whirled him around, snatched the gun out of his hands, and brought it down over her knee, cracking the handle.

Then she slapped Craig in the face as hard as she could.

I watched from the living room window, nursing my throbbing hand, tears streaming down my face.

"Gosh," I thought, "Sue must watch *The Rifleman*, too."

Chapter Nine

GUNS WERE a large part of our lives in Texas. Most of the time we used them to hunt. Tad, Craig, and I often headed out into the brush looking for "game."

In south Texas, that meant a snake, a raccoon, a possum, even a skunk.

It usually came down to snakes. They seemed to be all around us. But snakes can be dangerous. It's the big rattlesnakes ("rattlers" as we called them) you have to watch out for.

Our parents were always telling us about this or that child who reached into a hole to pull out a ball and lost a couple of fingers to a snake bite.

We knew better than to reach into a hole.

But you also had to watch where you stepped. Rattlers are lazy snakes. They like to sun themselves. They like to curl up on a rock and soak up the sun.

It was pretty easy to step on one because it blended in with the rocks. Fortunately, none of us ever stepped on a snake.

But we did get treed by some cows.

We were crossing a cow pasture one afternoon by Tad's house when we came upon a herd of cows huddled beneath a large tree. We must have spooked them because they started mooing and nudging each other.

Then the bull spied us and charged.

We ran as fast as we could to the nearest tree and climbed two-thirds up the trunk.

Just in time, too. The bull stood beneath the tree, shaking its horns and pawing at the ground.

Then, it just stood there.

There was nothing we could do but wait.

When it finally left, we climbed down the tree and headed home.

It was late afternoon. The sun slanted through the trees with a reddish-yellow glow.

Since we hadn't come upon anything to hunt, we were pretty bored. Tad and I were walking about fifty feet behind Craig, and, I don't know why, but I said...

"Hey, Tad, bet you can't hit Craig?"

"Shoot 'im?" Tad looked at me funny.

"Yeah," I replied with a grin.

Tad raised his BB gun and took a shot at Craig.

He missed.

I laughed and raised my BB gun and took a shot.

I missed, too.

Tad laughed and raised his gun again, but before he could get a shot off, Craig whirled around, raised his pellet gun to his hip, and started blasting away, just like the Rifleman.

Tad and I dove for cover. I landed on top of a small cactus. Tad cleared the cactus, but not one of Craig's pellets.

"Ouch!" he cried, rubbing the spot on his leg where the pellet hit him.

"Ya-ouch!" I cried, looking at the cactus thorns prickling my arm.

Then we rolled over on our backs and started laughing. When we finally got to our feet, Craig was nowhere in sight.

Chapter Ten

WE DID a lot of strange things in Texas, things that now, looking back, I cringe knowing how awfully stupid or just plain wrong they were.

Take the wars we waged: not with each other, but with the kids who lived about a mile away from us. They were the children of migrant workers, up from Mexico during the harvest season.

On a hot summer day, we'd gather our forces (which meant, Craig and Tad and I would meet in Craig's room and talk strategy).

Then, with our arsenal of weapons—two BB guns and a pellet gun—we'd make our way through the scrub brush to the edge of the field that bordered the migrant families' backyards, and wait.

We waited until there were enough kids out playing to enact our plans.

When the time was right we'd let out a bloodcurdling war whoop and burst out of the brush.

The girls in their thin frilly dresses would yell and scream and run into the house, while the boys picked up whatever was handy—rocks, sticks, empty bottles—and threw them at us as we ran by.

And run by we did, with guns a-blazing from the hip, Rifleman-style.

The fun of it wasn't so much hitting one of the migrant kids, as it was pretending to *be* the Rifleman.

We never questioned what we did. We never thought it was stupid, strange, or even wrong.

We just did it.

Our set was south Texas. The props were trees, bikes, fences, cars, and guns. The actors a strange mix of people and animals. Each of us played our role as we had learned it.

It was that simple.

Chapter Eleven

I DIDN'T ALWAYS hunt with Craig and Tad. Sometimes I went hunting with Wendell, my stepfather.

When I did, we didn't hunt in the backyard, or in the cow pastures surrounding our house. Wendell belonged to a hunting camp, and that's where we headed.

We'd arrive early, before the sun was up, and go directly to the camp's mess tent.

The mess tent was a large green army tent. On one side was the food line; on the other a cluster of tables. In the middle stood an iron wood-fired cook stove.

We'd pick up a plate and work our way down the

breakfast line, filling our plate with scrambled eggs, bacon, grits, and Mexican fry bread. Then we'd find a table and sit down and eat.

When we finished breakfast, we'd gather our gear and head out. But we rarely hunted together.

Rather, Wendell would deposit me somewhere—under a tree, in a clump of brush, or next to a dry creek bed—and then he'd head off to hunt by himself.

One morning he deposited me at the edge of a grove of trees with my mom's 20-gauge shotgun. He told me to stay put and look for doves. So I sat down on a log as Wendell drove off. He liked bigger game—turkey, wild boar, and deer.

It was late autumn. There was a coolness in the air that the morning sun hadn't burned off yet. I sat and waited for what seemed like an hour.

Finally, I heard a flutter of wings and the next thing I knew there was a large dove sitting on a branch in front of me. It couldn't have been more than five or six feet away from me. It just sat on the branch preening its feathers and cooing, oblivious to me.

I raised the barrel of the shotgun slowly, aimed, and squeezed the trigger. The gun fired with a loud *KA-BLAM,* knocking me off the log.

I scrambled to my feet and looked up. The dove was still sitting on the branch.

I couldn't believe it. *I missed!*

But as I looked closer, I realized I hadn't missed. Since the dove was so close to me, the shot from the gun hadn't had enough time to spread apart. So, when the shot hit the dove, it tore its head off, leaving its body teetering on the branch—until it fell lifelessly to the ground a few feet in front of me.

Chapter Twelve

MOST OF my life seems to have been one encounter after another, but the truth of it is there were a lot of open spaces between each encounter. Times when I was on my own and could think and dream.

My favorite getaway was in a small storage room off our carport. There were two rooms off the carport. The first one, closest to the backdoor, was the laundry room. That's where we kept the washer and dryer, a small portable clothesline, and two big freezers.

We had two freezers because my parents always bought a side of beef each year. That alone pretty much filled up one of the freezers. The other freezer had racks of dove and quail that we shot, as well as an assortment of other meat that we either killed or bought.

Next to the laundry room was a small storage room filled with stuff we no longer used—paint cans, bicycle parts, a set of old tires, a bed frame, an old mattress, a table, some chairs, and a shortwave radio.

I had folded the mattress over to make a small enclosure and pulled the radio up to close off the smaller of the two openings.

It was, in short, another fort, made for one—me.

I would lie there by the hour listening to the radio that brought in programs from around the world.

Half the time I had no idea what I was listening to because many of the programs weren't in English. But it didn't matter. I listened anyway.

I found the strange, exotic sounds intoxicating. What kind of people spoke like this? Where did they live? Were they surrounded by mesquite trees and scrub brush?

I had a burning desire to visit these foreign lands, to find out who these people were, to see how they lived.

But I would have to wait. For now I was stuck in a small town in south Texas.

Chapter Thirteen

OF COURSE, there were advantages of growing up in a small town. For one thing, you learned to drive a car at a younger age than most kids.

I started driving when I was nine.

I drove our riding lawn mower to cut our halfacre of grass. It was pretty easy to use: forward, backwards, and neutral. That's all there was to it. And since south Texas is as flat as the bottom of a frying pan, there really wasn't anything dangerous about it.

I guess that's why I thought I could drive Mom's car. She had a little metallic-blue Corvair, the kind with the engine in the back.

I remember the day. It was sweltering, the temperature pushing 95. I was all set to spend the day with my friend Tad who lived down the road about a quarter of a mile away.

I was going to ride my bike to Tad's house because we were going fishing at our favorite fishing hole. But when I went looking for my bike, it was gone.

I looked all around for it, but I couldn't find it anywhere. I stormed back into the house and found Sue in the kitchen.

"Do you know where my bike is?" I asked.

"Diane took it," she said, not looking up from clearing the breakfast table.

"Diane took it!" I yelled.

"Hey, she took mine, too," Sue huffed, "so don't yell at me."

Several of my oldest sister's friends had spent the night. When they got up in the morning they wanted to go to someone else's house and they took all the bikes in the carport, including mine.

I was furious. I really wanted my bike so I could go fishing with Tad. I went back outside and looked around.

No bikes, only Mom's Corvair. To me, it didn't look much different than the lawn mower.

So, without really thinking about it, I jumped into the car, turned on the engine (the keys were always in the ignition), and put the car in reverse. I backed out of the driveway, put the car in forward, and took off.

I drove down the dirt road to the main road and turned right, toward town.

It was surprisingly easy. I held onto the steering wheel with both hands, watched the road, and looked out of the mirrors occasionally.

I drove about a mile or two, and right before the turn-off into town I pulled into the parking lot of a small restaurant, where I turned around. Then, I headed back toward my house.

If only I had pulled into our driveway everything would have been all right. But I didn't. Instead, after turning off the main road, I kept going, thinking I'd drive the length of the dirt road that ran along our property before turning around.

It was the turn-around that did me in—and the dentist. First, the turn-around.

I tried to turn the car around on the dirt road, but the road was narrow and I backed into the barbed wire fence that ran along the road.

When I heard the *s-c-r-a-t-c-h* of the barbed wire scraping along the top of the trunk, I jammed on the brakes, put the car in park, and jumped out to see the damage I had done.

There were three deep scratches running up the trunk from the barbs in the fence. I was horrified. I was so shaken that I forgot to put the emergency brake down, which I must have pulled up before jumping out of the car.

The car wouldn't move, won't budge, not an inch, no matter what I did. I was stumped. So I left the car and walked home. But it wasn't the fact that I left the car stuck in the fence that got me in trouble. It was the dentist.

Chapter Fourteen

WE LIVED on "professional row." Our neighbors were an elite bunch: the town doctor, the dentist, the owner of the branch bank, and several other professional types.

It just so happened that while I was out driving on the main road, the dentist, who knew Mom (and her car), passed me driving in the opposite direction.

When he got home he called our house.

"Hello, Dorothy?" he asked, when Mom answered the phone.

"Yes," she said.

"It's Frank, down the block. The strangest thing just happened."

"What's that?" Mom asked.

"Well, I was driving home after some errands and I passed your little Corvair. But I swear no one was driving it."

"What?" Mom replied, dumbfounded.

"Yes," the dentist continued, "as your car passed me, I honked and gave a little wave, expecting that you'd do the same. But you didn't. No one did."

"I don't understand," Mom replied, completely dumbfounded.

"I swear there was no one driving your car," the dentist said, just as puzzled. "It's quite strange, don't you think?"

Before she could answer, I turned the doorknob and pushed the backdoor open. Mom turned and looked at me. I stopped dead in my tracks and looked around nervously.

Mom stared at me for a moment, then lowered the receiver and said, "You wait right there, young man!"

After she said good-bye to the dentist, she turned to me, the anger rising in her voice, and said, "Where have you been?"

"Uh, out," I said, staring at the floor.

"Out?" Mom echoed, looking past me to the spot in the carport where her car should have been parked.

"And *where* is my car?"

Chapter Fifteen

I'M SURE the dentist thought it was pretty strange to see a car drive by with no one in it. But then strange just seemed to be part of our world.

Craig, Tad, and I had a Sunday morning ritual. We would meet at Tad's house a little before noon and, following a dry creek bed, we'd head to a rundown house behind Tad's father's property.

It was owned by a family of Holy Rollers, reborn Pentecostal Christians who "spoke in tongues" while proclaiming their faith in God.

We'd sneak up to their property and watch them from a little rise next to the barn. That's where they met with several other families every Sunday morning.

They'd yell and scream, and roll around, flailing their arms and legs. This was their "service." There were no pews, no altar, no communion, no wine and bread—just a lot of rolling around and screaming.

It must have been entertaining because Craig and Tad and I made it our Sunday ritual to sneak up on them. But as strange as we thought they were, it was their son who caught our attention.

One Sunday, as we approached the house, we noticed him in the front yard. He wore a pair of pants—no shirt, no shoes, nothing, just a pair of pants torn off below the knees—and a target, a big red target that he had painted on his chest.

Curious, we stopped and watched him.

Using a hunting bow, he'd shoot an arrow high into the sky and then lay spread eagle on the ground and wait for it to come down.

The "game" was to see how close the arrow would come to him when it landed.

By itself, this was a really strange act, but it wasn't the whole scene. His dog, black as night with a white "cross" on its forehead, stood in a nearby tree.

Yes, that's right, *stood*.

It had managed to climb up the trunk, which was slanted at an angle. It just stood there, protective of its master, glaring at us.

A boy with a target on his chest...
A dog standing in a tree...
The screams of religious fanatics...
This was my world.
This was Texas.

Chapter Sixteen

TEXAS WASN'T only a strange place to grow up, it was also a tough place to grow up.

I remember we had a cat, a stray that had adopted us. We called it Smokey for its mottled blue-gray fur.

We didn't pay much attention to it. We fed it. That was about it. You'd see it around, then it would disappear for a few days, only to turn up again.

Once it disappeared for week. We thought it would come back. It always did. But after a week had passed we began to wonder where it was, what had happened to it.

We finally found it at the edge of our back yard, dead. Four holes, equally spaced, punctured its side. Someone had stabbed it with a pitchfork.

Yes, life could be tough at times.

My sister Sue loved animals, any animal, large or small. And she always seemed to have one—a dog, a couple of cats, a bird, a rabbit.

It was her rabbit, Black Jack, that she loved the most. She kept it in a cage outside. She cared for that rabbit like a mother cared for its child.

She fed it, watered it, and cleaned its cage. She even put a leash around its neck and took it for walks.

When the weather turned hot, she had to be very careful to move its cage out of direct sunlight, so Black Jack didn't get too hot.

One day she forgot. It was Sunday. We had plans to be out for the day.

Sue should have known better. She should have known that the sun would hit Black Jack's cage if she didn't move it before we left.

But she forgot.

When we got back, late that afternoon, Black Jack was dead. It lay in its cage with its water bowl overturned and its little blue-black tongue sticking out.

Sue cried all night.

Chapter Seventeen

TEXAS WASN'T just rough on animals.

Life with Wendell had its ups and downs, too. Mom married him several years after our father had died unexpectedly.

My sisters and I didn't like Wendell. He was strange. More than that, he was mean.

Our family ate together every night. Wendell at the head of the table. Mom nearest the kitchen. My sisters across the table from me.

Every night it was the same thing. We gathered around the table, each of us in his or her assigned seats.

There was no television. No radio. No soft music. No candles. Nothing. Dead quiet. Except for the occasional chit-chat between my sisters, or between Wendell and Mom.

In many respects, we were right out of the television show *Father Knows Best,* only the father we'd inherited was nothing like the father on television.

Wendell lacked not only warmth and humor; he also lacked any understanding of children. When we ate, there were several unspoken rules:

Don't talk unless spoken to...
Don't get up from the table unless you ask...
Don't play with your food...
and for me, and me alone:
Don't eat with your left hand...

I was the only person in our family who was lefthanded. For some reason Wendell got it into his head that I was never to eat using my left hand.

If I did, Wendell would clear his throat and glare at me until I switched hands, which I usually did.

If I didn't, he'd lean over the table and thump me on the head with the knuckle of his middle finger.

That usually took care of the eating-with-the-left-hand issue—but not always.

Sometimes impulse got the better of me.

Once, after being "corrected" several times for my lapse of memory, I reached for an extra piece of chicken with my left hand. I guess Wendell had had enough of thumping me on the head.

As my left hand neared the platter of chicken, Wendell leaned forward and drove his fork into the table a couple of inches ahead of my outstretched hand.

Mom gasped. My sisters froze. I quickly retracted my hand.

Wendell didn't flinch. He sat there glaring at me, like the neighbor's dog in the tree, holding onto the fork that he had driven into the table.

There are many things in my family that we never talk about: the four equally-spaced puncture marks in the dining room table is one of them.

Chapter Eighteen

WE DIDN'T talk about naptime either.

Yes, that's right. In our house we took naps—every Sunday afternoon.

I don't remember having breakfast together, or going to Church, or taking a Sunday afternoon walk. I just remember taking naps—or, more precisely, *trying* to take a nap.

In our house it wasn't enough to lie still during naptime, you had to be asleep. If you weren't, Wendell spanked you with his belt when he made his rounds.

Well, I was *never* asleep! I worried too much about being caught. It's not that I didn't have a strategy. I would lie down facing the wall, close my eyes, and clutch my favorite stuffed animal, a small sock monkey.

But when the door opened, every muscle in my body stiffened. If my sock monkey were a real monkey, I would have strangled it to death I tensed up so.

I'm sure there were other telltale signs of not being asleep because every Sunday afternoon it was the same.

"I said take a nap! And I mean it!"

Then *WHOMP* the belt came down on my backside—*WHOMP! WHOMP! WHOMP!*

Of course, I held it in—the pain, the fear, the outrage—until I heard the door close. Then I cried, but not too loud, for fear that Wendell would hear me.

Chapter Nineteen

SUNDAY AFTERNOON naptime was only one of our family rituals. Another was the family picnic.

If you're thinking a drive in the country, a large shade tree, and a picnic basket brimming with food, think again.

There was no country drive, no shade tree, no basket brimming with food. Our "picnic" was in the living room.

We spread a blanket in the middle of the floor. While my sisters and I ate bologna sandwiches on the blanket, and Mom ran back and forth between the kitchen and living room, Wendell sat in his green reclining chair, watching television.

It's funny what you remember looking back. We

must have had other furniture in the living room —besides the television and Wendell's green chair— but I don't remember any.

When I close my eyes and look around, I *only* see the green chair. It was his chair. No one else sat in it. We weren't allowed to, nor did we want to.

It was in that chair that we found the whip that Wendell used to hit us with, stuffed between the right arm of the chair and the worn seat cushion.

He bought it on a trip to Mexico. It wasn't one of those long leather-braided whips that cowboys crack for show at rodeos.

It was a small riding whip. Although he preferred the convenience of his belt, he'd also use the whip to hit us, probably more to scare us than anything.

So we feared it.

And that led to a little game between Wendell and my sisters and me. It was our version of the childhood game "Steal the Flag."

Two teams play the game. Each team has a home territory in which they hide a flag. Between the two territories is no-man's land. The team that finds the other team's flag first and can get it back to their territory wins.

Our game with Wendell was very similar.

Wendell would hide the whip and we would try to find it. When we did, we took it outside and buried it.

Wendell never said a thing. He just went out and bought another whip.

And the game started all over again.

Chapter Twenty

MAYBE I'M making too much of it all. Maybe it's just the way it is in Texas. Do something wrong and you pay for it.

That's the way it was in all those Westerns I watched. It didn't take long for the "bad guy" to land in jail, or, worse, get strung up, or shot.

That's the way it was around our house, too.

We had a dog named Bootsie. The ugliest dog you could ever imagine. Bootsie was a mutt—short, squat, a bit overweight, and really mangy.

Bootsie's favorite place to sleep in the summer was right up against the backdoor in the carport. When we ran the air conditioner on high, the cool air seeped out under the door and cooled the cement floor of the carport around the door.

Bootsie claimed this as her spot, and none of the other pets challenged her.

A familiar scene at our house on a hot summer day was Wendell trying to open the backdoor, and it wouldn't budge.

"Bootsie!" he'd yell, as he gave the door another push. On the other side of the door you'd hear a little yelp and the scurrying of paws across the carport floor.

One day Wendell pushed the door and it didn't budge. He yelled *"Bootsie!"* and tried again, but no luck. He tried again, and again. Finally, he put all of his might into it, yelling angrily, *"Bootsie!"*

Only, when the door opened, it wasn't Bootsie blocking the way, it was a six-foot rattlesnake that had taken Bootsie's place.

Wendell closed the door, walked to the master bedroom, and came out with his army service revolver. He exited the house using the back door, went around to the carport, walked up to the rattlesnake, and shot it point blank—one shot to the head.

You could argue that what Wendell did wasn't cruel. It was just how things were done in south Texas. It's how you survived.

After all, isn't that what growing up is all about—learning how to survive.

Chapter Twenty-one

I FELT like I had I learned how to survive the same way a dragonfly does.

A dragonfly spends almost two-thirds of its life underwater, first as an egg, then as a nymph, before it emerges from the water as an adult.

That's what I felt like.

I was underwater, underwater waiting, waiting for my wings, waiting to fly away.

But why did I have to wait?

Although we lived in a town full of ranchers, hired hands, and migrant workers, Wendell was none of these. He was a lawyer.

His father had been a lawyer as well. In fact, he had been the county attorney some years back.

Wendell was a cut above the rest, or so he thought. He also thought that someday he'd be the county attorney, just like his father.

But that was not to be.

For most of his practice Wendell had been the only lawyer in town. That changed when another lawyer moved to town—Harold, Craig's father.

It was okay at first. Wendell had his practice. Harold had his. Although they didn't get together socially, they weren't unfriendly toward each other either.

When the county attorney's position became vacant. Wendell put his name on the ballot.

So did Harold.

I don't remember much about the election, or the campaign leading up to it, but when it was over Wendell had lost.

It was at this point that our lives changed.

Wendell became moody, depressed. He had always been a drinker, but now he drank hard and often. He yelled more, cursed at every turn, and took his anger on us.

On me, my sisters, and Mom.

Chapter Twenty-two

I LEARNED about Mom's survival skills one day quite unexpectedly.

I was outside, cutting the grass in the backyard with our riding lawn mower. I loved mowing the lawn. It was just me, no one else, no one to tell me what to do.

If I wanted to turn left, I turned left. If I wanted to turn right, I turned right. I felt a degree of freedom that I didn't feel anywhere else.

That's how it was going this day, just me, alone in my thoughts—*and then it happened!*

The mower's rotary blades picked up a rock and hurled it with Olympian force through the plate-glass sliding door at the back of our house.

The glass broke with a resounding crash. Total annihilation. There were glass shards everywhere.

Mom heard it and came running. She stood there horrified. Not at what I had done, but at what Wendell would say—*and do*—when he got home from work.

We did not have to wait long to find out.

Wendell came home shortly afterwards. When he walked into the house he immediately sensed something was wrong. When he found out what I had done, he went through the roof.

"Where is he? Where is he?" he kept saying. *"I'll kill him!"*

I knew he meant it.

Reluctantly, Mom said that I was in my room.

And I was, cringing behind the door, listening to Wendell yelling uncontrollably.

"Get him!" he ordered, *"Get him!"*

When Mom found me, she took my hand and walked me into the living room.

Wendell was already taking off his belt (there was no time for the whip). *"I'll kill him! I'll kill him!"* he yelled over and over again.

Then, it happened...

Mom, who always stepped between us, between Wendell and me, or between Wendell and my sisters, began to yell at me just as loudly.

"No, I'll kill him!" she said. *"I'll kill him!"*

As she yelled, she grabbed the belt out of Wendell's hand and dragged me back into my room.

She slammed the door, led me across the floor, and sat me down on my toy chest. Then she bent over and whispered in my ear—

"Scream!"

I started screaming at the top of my lungs as Mom belted the top of the toy chest with Wendell's belt. The harder she swung, the louder I screamed.

It's funny what you think about in times of great duress. I couldn't help but think about that dragonfly, the one Craig had mutilated.

If only I had stepped between it and Craig.

If only I had inserted myself into the situation—been strong enough, courageous enough, like Mom—perhaps it would still be alive.

Chapter Twenty-three

THE BEST memories—and the worst—are often frozen in one's mind, etched there for life, whether or not they actually happened.

I don't know if the memory of the last time I saw Wendell actually happened or not.

I've never asked Mom or my sisters if it did. But it remains for me one of the clearest images that I have of him.

It was late one afternoon, not too long after the lawn mower incident. My parents were in their bedroom, fighting.

Usually, during one of their fights, I'd find my sisters and stay close to them, until the fury ended.

So, when the fighting began, I ran to my sisters'

room, which was next to my parents' room, but it was empty. As I turned to run back to my room, the door to my parents' bedroom suddenly flew open.

I was caught, like a deer in the headlights, in the hallway just outside their room.

The room itself didn't surprise me: my sisters and I had explored it before, when our parents were out of the house.

It was your typical ranch-style bedroom: a large bed butted up against the longest wall, framed by a nightstand on either side, a bureau hugged the opposing wall between two closet doors.

What struck me was not how large the room was, but how dark it was. A set of thick green curtains adorning the windows seemed to suck all of the light out of the room.

The darkness was made even more oppressive by the heaviness of the furniture: each piece made out of a knotty, dark-grained wood.

On this particular afternoon, when the door opened, I didn't look at the room itself.

I looked at Mom: she was crying.

But it wasn't her tears that caught my attention. It was the tortured look on her face.

Although my parents were fighting, it was eerily quiet. Not that they weren't making any sounds. There were plenty of sounds—yelling, scuffling, crying.

It's just that the sounds they made seemed to pass through my mind without it registering them. What I did register was my mom's tortured face.

And the gun...

Mom ran past me first, followed by Wendell, who waved his service revolver in the air.

That's when the audio kicked back on.

"I'll kill you!" he shouted as he chased her, waving the gun in the air. *"I'll kill you!"*

A familiar refrain in our household, but for some reason the words held more meaning this time, and fear. They ran down the hallway, but I couldn't tell you *where* they ran to. I don't remember.

I just remember
    the yelling...
        the tears...
            the gun...

Chapter Twenty-four

It was not long after that, maybe a few days, a week (though it could have been just a matter of hours), that we left.

Mom hurried us into the Corvair. She threw a couple of bags in the trunk, stuffed the backseat with pillows and blankets, put me in the front seat, my sisters in the back. And we were off.

Where? I didn't know at the time. All I knew was we were off—Mom, my sisters, and me.

We drove all day. By the look of the sun we were headed east. My grandmother had a beach house in Florida, maybe that's where we were going.

We stayed overnight in a small motel, where we

begged Mom to let us swim in the motel swimming pool.

At night we jumped from bed to bed and had a pillow fight, while Mom stared at the television with red, swollen eyes.

We headed out early the next morning.

For some reason I still commanded the front seat. My sisters preferred the back seat, where they lay claim to a fortress of pillows and blankets.

While they slept, I gazed out the window, occasionally turning to steal a glimpse of Mom's face.

She wasn't crying any more, but the dark lines in her face kept her tortured past alive.

And mine, too.

I kept seeing
>   *the whip...*
>   *the belt...*
>   *the fork...*
>   *the gun...*

I couldn't get them out of my mind.

But I saw other things, too: Tad's horses, our tree

forts, my favorite fishing hole, Craig's backyard, my bicycle.

As these and other images flashed through my mind, Mom pulled the car into a small picnic area.

"Time to stretch your legs," she said wearily, as she opened the car door and climbed out.

"Get out?" I thought.

"What if he's chasing us?"

"What if he's right behind us?"

"What if he catches us?"

As these thoughts flooded my mind, a dragonfly landed on the mirror outside my window.

I studied it for a moment, and then slowly, carefully, rolled down the window. The dragonfly fluttered and buzzed, but it didn't fly away.

I reached out very slowly and put my fingertips on the mirror just below the dragonfly.

More fluttering, more crackling and buzzing, but still it didn't fly away.

I slid my fingers a little higher, then with a quick motion I caught one set of the dragonfly's wings.

It flapped its free wings with all of its might, but I caught that set too with my other hand.

I held it in my hands—one set of wings in my left hand, the other set in my right.

I kept the wings taut, stretched to their fullest.

The dragonfly twitched and buzzed, trying to escape my hold.

Slowly, I raised it to the sunlight and inspected it—the silvery, translucent wings, the bluish-green body, the large, bulbous eyes.

Then I lowered it.

For a moment I thought about what would happen if I pulled my hands apart. What would happen if I stretched those wings beyond their limit.

But I knew what would happen.

I knew from the few short years I had lived in south Texas what happens when you stretch something beyond its breaking point.

So, with the morning breeze washing my face, my sisters asleep in the backseat, and Mom silhouetted against the trees, I opened my hands and relaxed my fingers.

At first, the dragonfly didn't move.

Then, with a crackle and a buzz, it lifted off my hand, hovered in midair, and flew away.

It was free. *Free!*

And so was I.

About the Author

W. Nikola-Lisa is the author of numerous books for readers young and old, including *Bein' With You This Way, Shake Dem Halloween Bones*, and *How We Are Smart*. An accomplished storyteller and musician, Mr. Nikola-Lisa travels to schools and libraries throughout the country to share his writing and publishing experiences. For more information about his books or author programs, visit the author on the web at www.nikolabooks.com.

If you liked *Dragonfly*, then you might also enjoy these books by the author:

 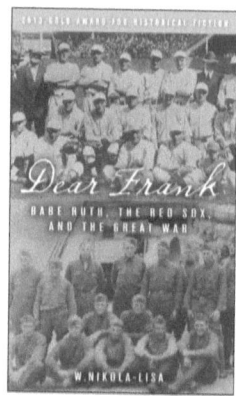

All books available on Amazon, Barnes & Noble, IndieBound, and other online retailers of your choice.

For more information, visit gyroscopebooks.com

www.ingramcontent.com/pod-product-compliance
Lightning Source LLC
Chambersburg PA
CBHW021135300426
44113CB00006B/439